T3-BOR-619

LIVING HAPPILY EVER LAUGHTER

LIVING HAPPILY EVER

LAUGHTER

A Guide to Thinking Funny
in a *Fast* Paced World

by
Kathy Brown

illustrated by Heidi Brandt

Beaver's Pond Press
Edina, Minnesota

Text and Illustration copyright © 1997 by Kathy Brown
All rights reserved. No part of this book may be reproduced or
utilized in any form or by any means, electronic or mechanical,
including photo copying, recording, or by any other information
storage and retrieval system, without permission in writing from
Kathy Brown.

ISBN 1-890676-00-4

Printed in the United States of America.

J   I   H   G   F   E   D   C   B   A

To order additional copies contact:

Kathy Brown & Associates
612/730-1109 fax: 612/578-8265
P.O. Box 25744
Woodbury, Minnesota 55125

Production Coordination by Milton E. Adams

Dedicated to
Those Who Love To Laugh
especially
Ken
for his love and encouragement

AND

Jeff, Julie & Steve

My three "near-perfect" children
who make my heart soar
and my face laugh

Introduction

"Living Happily Ever Laughter … A Guide To Thinking Funny In A *Fast* Paced World" was written to motivate you to laugh more in a world that is often discouraging. Laughter has proven therapeutic value with no side effects. This book was designed and written to be fun to read, yet thought provoking to challenge you to look inward and upward. Humor is all around us if we will take the time to explore the less obvious.

It is my sincere desire that you will find some positive life applications within these pages. In your quest for success you will find that laughter is good for business. May you live in the light of love and travel this world on the wings of laughter.

If you don't like to laugh, at least smile.
People will wonder why.
This can lead to some great
conversations.

Have you ever wondered why
some people don't laugh?

*"The results came back positive. I'm afraid
you ARE a jerk."*

A cheerful heart does good like medicine,
but a broken spirit makes one sick.

—Proverbs 17: 22

Some people resist laughing because they think it's not professional and they won't be taken seriously. The truth is:
"He who laughs … lasts."

Humor is an attitude. Good humor
is being at ease with yourself.
Happiness is a skill to be developed.

Where did you "Hide Your Happy" today?

A smile can light up a room.

Humor is a "Funny" thing. It is really all around us if we look at things through the eyes of our inner child.

Life can be a real "gas."

People with a sense of humor are more effective leaders and better team players. There is also less turnover when people enjoy the people they work with.

Hire the Happy.

They are more "fun" to work with.

If you can't be happy with what you have
you will not be happy when you get
what you think you want.

Celebrate the "Present." It is a gift.

Don't be like the person who lights up
the room when he/she leaves.
Think and Be Positive.
Positive people attract others.

*Put on a Happy Face. It is more
important to have fun
than to be funny.*

How you spend your time, with whom,
and doing what shows
what you really value.

Dust is not dirt.

*It is merely a protective coating
for your furniture.*

Stress happens when your stressors are greater than your resources.

If Moses came down from the mountain right now, the two tablets he'd be carrying would be aspirin.

Your work is a way of discovering
yourself. People work for a
number of different reasons.

"I owe, I owe … so off to work I go."

Repeated "requests" can become annoying. Being creative and a little playful can make all the difference.

Don't fight ... write.

*Not caring enough to say something could be
a "hair raising" experience.*

You must <u>Be</u> and <u>Do</u>
before you <u>Have</u>.

Americans spend money they don't have on things they don't need to impress people they don't know.

"Look at me!"

What gives us our identity in life?
Substance or "stuff?"

When Fear knocks on your door … send Faith to answer it … and there won't be anyone there.

"Is anyone there?"

*Feel the fear and do it anyway.
Push through your fear into
your potential.*

It is possible to give without loving, but it is impossible to love without giving.

Cash in before you "cash out."

The REAL living is in the giving!

Hard work pays off later, but laziness pays off now.

Work can be a "remote" experience.

House cleaning never killed anyone ...but why take the chance?

Often more success can be found
by digging deeper where you
are than by taking your
shovel and digging
across the street.

Showing up in life where you
should be, and on time,
pays rich dividends.

"Be there ... or Beware"

Absence can make the work grow longer.

The clever use of words can be charming, and confusing.

I know there's a message here ...

The best way to succeed in life is to act on the advice we give to others.

It's a sad world but we don't need
to let the sad world live in us.

SMILE ... and let the world wonder why.

Of all the things you wear ... your expression is the MOST important.

Hugs are all natural with no preservatives or artificial ingredients. There are no batteries to wear out, no monthly payments … and they are fully returnable.

Hugs happen ... but not often enough!

Go ahead. Make my day.

Take time to listen to others.
Be a listener worth speaking to.
People having mood swings
need listeners who care.

We all need caring listeners, especially when we're "weird."

It's what inside each one of us that makes us truly beautiful.

Don't feel bad when hair starts to thin or you get bald spots.

Remember: They don't put marble tops on cheap furniture.

We're ALL a little dysfunctional BUT, there's even "fun" in the word … dysFUNctional.

There is NO evidence that the tongue is connected to the brain.

How you act Today
determines your Future.

*"You cannot become what you need to be
by remaining where you are"*

—Bill McGee

Some people just don't "get it."

First I was dying to finish
high school and start college.
And then I was dying to finish
college and start working.
And then I was dying to marry
and have children.
And then I was dying for my
children to grow old enough
for school so I could return to work.
And then I was dying to retire.
And now, I AM dying …
and suddenly I realize
that I forgot to live.

–ANON

People who take themselves
lightly are likable.

Love laughs together.

If you are liked, you can do wrong and people will still care about you.

Are you afraid that if you are not constantly busy you will not be successful? Being productive in achievement, financial success and having a clean house can happen while you are personally falling apart.

The USA is the only nation that has
a Mount "Rush More."

Attitudes are contagious.
Is yours worth catching?

Some people are professional
lemon tasters.

It all started when someone got off the
MAYFLOWER in a bad mood.

Do our children see differences in
what we say and how we live?
Is success more important
than happiness or is happiness
the real measure of success?

When we become happy parents
our children will become
happy children.

You can't microwave relationships.

Often what we "really" want is hidden beneath what we have settled for.

You have to know yourself before you can share that self with someone else.

Unconditional love lasts.

A marriage may be made in heaven but the maintenance must be done on earth.

Have you ever looked back at a
time in your life and thought
"I was really happy then. It's
too bad I didn't realize it
so I could have enjoyed
it more."

Keep asking yourself, what "really" matters?

It's never too late to say "I'm sorry."
Awareness + Forgiveness = Happiness.

Humor brings our differences together
and makes something beautiful …
like a Smile.

This body was built for comfort,
NOT for speed.

Experience is the
intelligent use of mistakes.
Recovery is just an insight away.

Give people "Freedom to Fail."

It has been said that all things come to those who wait, but it's what is leftover from those who hustle.

We create our world from our thoughts and actions. We reap what we sow.

Kindness is Contagious!

It is impossible to find happiness
through trying to prove your
own self importance.

Win or lose, our value as a person remains.
We're ALL important.

When we are nice because it feels
like the natural thing to do,
we experience satisfaction
and contentment.

Modern version of chivalry

There is true joy in doing for others. No strings attached.

Definition of intelligence:
the wisdom to be happy no matter
what other people think.

A quiet mind is the best cure for a low mood. When you are quiet, you can access wisdom, common sense, and inspiration.

Your perceptions become your realities.
You become what you think about.

Want to increase your face value?
<u>Smile</u>. Laughter <u>loves</u> company!

Want to make GOD laugh?

Tell Him "your" plans.

"Platinum rule: do unto others as THEY want done unto them."

—Tony Alessandra, Ph.D.

Respect one another's thoughts and possessions.

*Healthy conflict can be fun if you both
have a good sense of humor.*

When you throw dirt at someone,
YOU are the one that's
losing ground.

Two things are hard on the heart—running <u>up</u> stairs and running <u>down</u> people.

It's your attitude, not your aptitude, that determines your altitude in life.

*Humility and Humor make
a great combination.*

"It is not only what we do, but also what we do not do, for which we are accountable."

—Moliere

You know the day will only get better
when the first thing you hear in
the morning is …

*Untimely observations in life can
lead to unfortunate outcomes.*

The greatest thing we can do for ourselves and our relationships is to be happy.

Do the things that make you happy.

In the amount of time it takes for
the mind to invent a good
excuse, it could have
created an alternate
way of achieving
the desired result.

*Train a child in the way he should
go and when he is old he
will not turn from it.*

—Proverbs 22:6

Children ARE the Future

*When a "stay at home" mom or daycare
provider is asked,
"and what do you do?" say
"I'm an investment broker.
I'm into <u>FUTURES</u>."*

Being too busy for others keeps
us isolated. Relationships are
what ground us in what
really matters.
Together Everyone
Accomplishes More.
(T-E-A-M)

"O. K. Let's try to get a date on the calendar
when we can meet."

Worry is like a rocking chair.
It's something to do, but
you're not going anywhere
or solving anything.

*I wish I had an odometer
on this thing.*

We keep some habits far longer than
it's healthy for us to do so.
A negative habit can
make you sick.

If something walks out of your refrigerator …
let it go.

Are you fun to be around?
Allow your inner child to
come out and play when
it's appropriate. Find out
your "fun factor."

Oops! An idea got stuck.

*I act weird so that other
people will feel normal.*

You become what you think about
(or sing about).

Ballad: Elvis is dead … and I don't feel so good myself.

A little levity helps people relax.
It relieves tension and builds
communication.

Relief isn't always in the medication.

Feed your relationships by sharing
your thoughts, dreams ...
and desserts.

When you first fall in love you feed each other. After marriage, you protect your food.

Choose your battles.
Know what hill to take a stand on.

Children fight over less
important issues.

*Youth is a temporary condition
from which one usually recovers.*

Inflation lets you live in a
better neighborhood without
going through the bother
of moving.

No matter what your lot in life is …
… build something on it.

Success is in the eyes of the beholder.
A house becomes a home when it is filled
with love and laughter.

Sometimes we are so busy adding up
our troubles that we forget to
count our blessings.

Be a Blessing to Someone TODAY!

About the Author

Kathy Brown is a nationally recognized keynote speaker and seminar leader who brings a dynamic and fun approach to each of her customized presentations. Her background brings a wealth of information turned into practical steps to go from pain to power on the wings of laughter.

For information about Kathy's presentations, contact:

Kathy Brown & Associates
(612) 730-1109 • fax (612) 578-8265
e-mail: Kbrown471@aol.com

About the Illustrator

Heidi Brandt is presently a graphic arts student in the process of ultimately receiving a master's degree in illustration. She is a "regular" as a caricature artist at the Valleyfair Amusement Park and at Camp Snoopy at the Mall of America.

NAME _____

ADDRESS _____

CITY _____ STATE _____ ZIP _____

Quantity

_____ **"Living Happily Ever Laughter:** $ _____
NEW! **A Guide To Thinking Funny In
A Fast Paced World."**
$7.95, plus $2.50 S/H = $10.45

_____ **"How To Live Happily** $ _____
Ever Laughter"
full color 1 hr. video tape
$29.95, plus $4.95 S/H = $34.90

_____ **"How To Live Happily Ever Laughter"**
1 hr. audio tape
$10.00, plus $2.50 S/H = $12.50

_____ **"Give Your Life A Lift"** $ _____
1 hr. audio tape
SPECIAL $5.00, plus $2.50 S/H = $7.50

MN residents add 6.5% sales tax $ _____

TOTAL $ _____

Payment by: Check _____ Visa _____ MasterCard _____

Print name as it appears on card _____
Signature _____
Card number _____ Expiration Date _____

☐ I would like more information on Kathy Brown's presentations. A 10-minute color videotape and media packet is available upon request.